Banza's Incredible Journey

and other stories from ADRA

Celeste perrino Walker

Pacific Press Publishing Association
Boise, Idaho
Oshawa, Ontario, Canada

Edited by Bonnie Tyson-Flyn
Designed by Dennis Ferree
Cover art by Lars Justinen from ADRA photos
Typeset in Caslon 224 Book 11/13

ISBN 0-8163-1278-8

99 98 97 96 95 • 1 2 3 4 5

Contents

Foreword

As I got out of the Italian army helicopter, I looked on a large group of Somalis dressed in their best garb. I later learned that these were the elders of the community who had come to welcome us. We had been working in Adale for some time, and Dr. Hugo Sosa had won the friendship and admiration of the elders. Hugo was considered a great man. He brought not only medical care and health but hope to a region devastated by civil war. Now I was the object of their interest. In their minds, somebody bigger than Hugo was coming to their village by the sea. They were out to impress me.

But what caught my eye the moment I set foot in the clinic was a woman holding a sick child on her lap. She wasn't crying; she didn't look desperate. Yet I could tell her child was very ill. I went directly to her and, with the help of Abdulai Ali, a Somali doctor, talked to her.

"That's a beautiful child you have."

"Yes," was her only reply.

"Is she ill?"

"She hasn't eaten in three days. She can't keep anything down."

"You came to the right place," I reassured her. There seemed to be a slight glimmer of hope in her eyes. When

Hugo joined us, her demeanor changed completely.

"Doctor, you can help her; I know you can." There was expectation in her voice and face. She turned to me. "Are you also a doctor? The doctor we had before Hugo couldn't do anything to help us."

"A witch doctor," Hugo interpreted for me.

"No, I'm not a doctor. Sometimes I wish I were. But I can do something to help. I can keep Hugo here for as long as you need him. Actually, we're sending a full team of doctors to help Hugo."

"Can you do that?" It was as if a great burden had lifted from her shoulders. "May God bless you forever."

I didn't see that woman again. I don't know her name. But I have felt as if her blessing has been with me these years since we had that brief conversation. God has blessed me and has blessed our work.

I want to share who we are and what we do. You see, I'm the president of a worldwide organization. We call it *ADRA*. It's short for *Adventist Development and Relief Agency*. We do two things at ADRA: we do relief, and we do development. ADRA has offices in more than eighty countries. Some of those offices implement work similar to what Dr. Sosa has done in Somalia. Other offices provide funding and resources for development and relief work to take place, such as the work ADRA has conducted in Rwanda. Offices in Germany, Australia, Denmark, and Italy—to name a few—contributed to efforts in Rwanda, so devastated by civil war.

ADRA's roots reach back nearly eighty years. In 1918, just after World War I, the Seventh-day Adventist denomination established a committee to assist church workers, missionaries, and members in need as a result of war. Among the first countries and areas to receive aid were Belgium, France, Germany, Turkey, Egypt, the Middle East, Russia, and China.

Foreword

Then World War II came. The devastation in Europe, North Africa, and parts of Asia again called for immediate attention. The Adventist Church established warehouses in New York and San Francisco to process materials to ship overseas.

In 1956 the General Conference of Seventh-day Adventists created the Seventh-day Adventist Welfare Service, Incorporated (SAWS). The name was modified in 1973 to Seventh-day Adventist World Service, and in 1983 SAWS was reorganized under the current name. The goal was to provide better management for the agency and to put more emphasis on development issues and organizational development. In 1985 I joined ADRA as president. Since then, the agency has grown in magnitude, commitment, and dedication to development and relief issues.

The Adventist Church demonstrates its commitment to helping people through an agency such as ADRA, which provides humanitarian relief during times of disaster and stays on for long-term development.

When disaster strikes, ADRA gives food, clothing, blankets, emergency shelter, and medical aid to people who need it most. After the shock has passed, ADRA stays to rebuild communities and lives that have been nearly destroyed. I have visited houses ADRA helped rebuild on Corn Island, off the coast of Nicaragua, after a hurricane destroyed all the houses on that tiny island. I have visited a medical clinic in the Turkish mountains where ADRA doctors provided medical care to Kurdish refugees after the Persian Gulf War. I visited ADRA's relief work in the parks of Los Angeles following the 1994 earthquake. ADRA's relief work has often led to development work. A new village replaces the one a volcano destroyed in Armero, Colombia, in South America. And these are just a few examples. I could write about many more.

However, disaster relief is only part of ADRA's mission. ADRA shares other goals that the Adventist Church has always emphasized. One of these goals is health care and education. ADRA builds and supplies many clinics, hospitals, and schools.

For example, consider Malamulo Hospital in Malawi, in southeastern Africa. The hospital—one of the church's largest in Africa—was founded in 1902 and has recently been rebuilt. The goal of the hospital is not only to take care of the sick but also to bring a better way of life to surrounding communities.

Malamulo Hospital, cooperating with ADRA, operates outreach programs to outlying communities. Clinics are set up for children under the age of five. Mothers take their babies to the clinics for immunization. While there, they learn about nutrition and how to better care for their children. "Under-5" clinics located in local communities are essential to children's health. Without such clinics, children are not immunized and will fall to illness that could easily be prevented.

Since 1986, the hospital, working with ADRA, has dug 120 wells in the surrounding areas. Easy access to clean water means improved health for everyone and reduces the infant mortality rate.

ADRA has also secured grants, through various international donors, to build and supply an operating theater, a new ward for children, a nursery, rooms for short-term patients, and a new dining room for Malamulo Hospital.

Education, another area the church emphasizes, is a part of ADRA's mission. In 1977 the Adventist Mission in Burkina Faso, a small country in western Africa, built a large market-gardening training center in Bazega. The goal: to train farmers to be self-sufficient and to improve the quality of nutrition by teaching market-gardening skills.

Foreword

Each year, twenty trainees, representing ten villages, attend the training center for seven months. The trainees receive room and board and even medical treatment. At the conclusion of the course, they receive materials they need to start a garden.

Students attend classes for six hours daily. Two hours are theory, and four hours are practical training. They learn market gardening, irrigation, bookkeeping, nutrition, and soil preparation. At the conclusion of the course, teachers accompany the students to their villages to help them get started.

These classes have had a very positive side effect. As ADRA proved to the villagers of Bazega that they were there to help, an atmosphere of trust developed between ADRA and the community. Just over a year ago, the first Seventh-day Adventist church was dedicated on the campus of the training center. Its existence is a direct result of ADRA's work in the community. The church has a 200-seat capacity, but on the day of the dedication, more than 300 adults and children joined the celebration.

As mentioned earlier, the health of mothers and children is one of ADRA's primary concerns. It holds clinics to stress growth monitoring, oral rehydration therapy, breast-feeding, and immunization. At these clinics, parents learn nutrition, hygiene, child spacing, and child care. ADRA also provides supplemental food aid to pregnant women, nursing mothers, and preschool children. A combination of all these activities greatly improves mothers' and children's health.

ADRA operates a variety of agricultural programs that emphasize better food production for better nutrition and income generation. Farmers in Zimbabwe, Africa, have been learning techniques to grow more viable gardens. The program is widely recognized as one of the most effective in all of Africa. Self-sufficiency among farmers improves the quality of life in a community.

Developing water resources is a key element in ADRA's development projects. Clean water means less disease, better hygiene, and better health. In 1994 four million children died from diarrhea, a direct result of not having access to clean water. Many of these deaths could have been prevented had clean water been available.

For women who normally walk several miles each day for water, a well in their home village means more time to take care of children or work in the garden. Developing clean water resources is essential to a community's well-being.

ADRA also distributes food aid to hungry people. ADRA will work with community leaders in an impoverished village to find out what the people need. Many times it is a school, a road, or a community center. Workers are paid with food to build what is needed. The entire community reaps the rewards, not only by additional food, but when the project is completed, the people have something that benefits the community.

The Adventist Church has commissioned ADRA for a very special mission. That mission is to help the most needy of God's children. The task seems nearly impossible at times, but with God's help, ADRA continues to feed the hungry, clothe the naked, and shelter the homeless. ADRA continues to express God's love in concrete ways to His needy children.

Yes, I have been blessed by the words of that Somali woman. But more important, her child—and many other lives—are being blessed and helped because of ADRA's work.

Ralph S. Watts, Jr.
President, ADRA International

Amidst
the
Slaughter

The phone rang just as Carl Wilkens, ADRA's director of operations in Rwanda, was pushing his chair back from the table. His wife, Theresa, paused a moment from gathering the dishes off the table. Carl waved a hand.

"That's OK," he told her. "I'll get it."

He immediately recognized the voice of one of his friends from the university on the other side of the country.

"Can you see the fire?" the man asked excitedly.

Carl covered the mouthpiece of the phone and smiled at Theresa's questioning look. "It's just Bob. He wants to know if we can see the fire."

Theresa grinned. "Why? Is he trying to cook supper again?"

Carl chuckled. "Theresa wants to know if you are trying to make your famous burritos. You know, the ones that are black on the outside and cold on the inside."

Bob's voice was urgent, almost frantic. "I'm not fooling around, Carl. Didn't you hear? Their plane crashed."

Carl scrambled to grasp what Bob was saying. "Theirs? Whose? Whose plane crashed?"

"The presidents of Rwanda and Burundi. It's just a few miles from your house."

Carl hung up the receiver and dashed to the window. Theresa followed, alerted by the stunned expression on Carl's face. Together they scanned the darkened landscape for any sign of fire, praying that the news reports were false or inflated.

"There." Theresa pointed a trembling finger in the direction of a faint orange glow. Carl took her hand and squeezed it. They had been married for thirteen years, arriving in Africa six weeks after their wedding. They had lived there ever since.

Having passed through some perilous times while living in Zimbabwe, where foreigners were sometimes the target of ambushes and other dangers, Rwanda at first had seemed like a paradise in comparison. For their family, Rwanda had been a great place to live. The climate was nice, and they always found places to go camping. Their first six months of peace in Rwanda was followed abruptly by the outbreak of war. But the war was far removed. Until . . .

"What do you think will happen?" Theresa asked softly. Carl knew her thoughts were on their three children playing in the other room.

Carl shrugged, trying not to let her see how worried he was. "I suppose they'll shut down the city for a couple days. I don't know what else. Why don't you go get the kids, and we'll pray."

Carl woke with a start as a bomb fell particularly close to the house. He could hardly believe he'd fallen asleep again. The incessant pounding of his heart echoed in his ears. He tried to pull the mattress over himself more tightly.

This had turned into what Carl had begun to refer to as a "two-mattress night." When the bombing was exceptionally heavy, he dragged two mattresses into the hallway, away from the shattered windows and debris. Lying on one, he pulled the other on top of himself for protection.

"What kind of protection is that?" a friend who was the head of the Red Cross in Kigali had asked him. "Does your house have a concrete roof?"

"No," Carl had told him. "Our roof is just asbestos sheets."

"Man, you should move into a house with a concrete roof," his friend had urged.

"I am right where God wants me to be," Carl insisted. "I'm in the safest place possible—in the hands of God."

"Well, your life may be in the hands of God, but those bombs—I don't think the Lord is directing those bombs."

Carl had to assume that the Lord was indeed directing the bombs, since none had landed on the house with the asbestos roof so far.

The bombing ceased for a little while, and Carl felt his eyelids growing heavy. He had grown so accustomed to the bombings that most nights he could sleep right through. But tonight, for some reason, every little sound startled him. Being wakened every half-hour made the night interminable. Soon the bombing would start again, and he needed every bit of sleep he could get. Slowly, he drifted off.

The sound of gunfire woke Carl, and by the time he struggled into a sitting position, Theresa was already drawing all the shades. Carl pushed himself out of bed and went to get the kids.

"Let's pretend we're camping," he suggested.

"Daddy?" Five-year-old Shawn's eyes were wide with fear. "What's happening? Are we in the war?"

Carl pulled the boy into his arms, and the two girls, Mindy and Lisa, crowded around too. "It looks like it, Shawn. But remember what we said earlier? God will take care of us."

"What's going to happen to us?" Mindy asked, her expression much too serious for a child of ten. Lisa, two years younger, poked her in the side.

"Nothing's going to happen, silly. Daddy just said that God will take care of us."

"Everything will be fine," Carl heard himself say.

Except that it wasn't.

The next day brought more tragedies—a crisis at the orphanage, then one at the university. Carl spent the entire day in frantic communication by radio and telephone with the embassy, the university, the orphanage, and the hospital. By the time the day was over, the telephone lines were dead, leaving him with only the radio.

By Sunday morning, two short days after the plane crash, the United States government was preparing to shut down the embassy, urging all American citizens to leave the country. The last chance for any assistance from the U.S. government was leaving with the last convoy carrying the ambassador and the remainder of the embassy staff out of the country.

Another bomb blast wakened Carl. He heard the tinkle of shattering glass close by. It was amazing. On the days he was able to move around the city, he observed that some buildings were flattened or completely looted, and then almost next to them were buildings with only one broken pane of glass. He told Theresa about it during their daily radio communications.

Thinking about Theresa brought on fresh waves of loneliness. One of the hardest things he had ever done was watch Theresa and the children leave with the convoy after he signed documents stating that he had turned down the help of the United States government by choosing to remain in Rwanda.

"Daddy has to stay and help the orphans," he had overheard Theresa telling Mindy and Lisa again as they waited in line. Shawn clung to Teresa's leg, silent tears rolling down his cheeks. "The orphans have some serious problems, and they need Daddy's help," she told the children.

Carl drifted off to sleep again.

Even mingled with the static, Theresa's voice over the radio warmed Carl's heart. It had been one week since the evacuees had sought the safe haven of Burundi. The transmission faltered, and Carl lost part of what Theresa was saying.

"Repeat that," he requested.

"I said that things here are getting unstable. We're not sure if Burundi is going to explode like Rwanda did. We're going to move on to Nairobi. The others are talking about going on to the States."

Carl swallowed hard. Was any place safe anymore? "I think you should go to the States with them," he said quietly.

"No," Theresa replied firmly. "I'm not going to America. It's too far. At least in Nairobi I can still talk to you on the radio. If there's anything I can do, I'll be here to give support. I'll be as close as possible."

Carl rolled over and squinted out between the two mattresses. Daylight filtering in through the broken window brought with it fragments of the dreams he'd been having all night. How many times before this was over would he relive everything that had happened since the fateful night of the plane crash? Sometimes he wondered if he even had the strength to think about it. But somehow God always provided the strength he needed.

Each morning brought the reality of war back to him as fresh as if he were learning about it for the first time. Mornings like this when shadows of dreams plagued him, it was hard to remember all the miraculous ways God had been with him since the violence had started. It was hard to see God's hand leading.

Inside, his stomach twisted in knots. He wanted to get up, but he was afraid his legs would buckle under him. He did not want to go out today. But there were people depending on him, not only for care, food, and physical safety, but also for the encouragement he was providing by just remaining in the country when other Americans had left.

Carl crawled onto his knees, hunkered beneath the mattress. He bowed his head. "Dear Lord, I don't want to enter this day without coming before You in thanks for the help You've given me in the past. We've been through some pretty hairy experiences, and I don't want to forget what's happened and how You delivered us. You know that we must pass through the militia barriers today. I don't know how I'm going to face that again, but I have faith that You'll bring me through again like You've done before.

"I'm placing my life—and the life of my wife and kids—in Your hands, Lord. You love my wife. You love my kids more than I ever could, and if I'm not there to provide for them, You have a way to do it even better than I. Thank You for Your love and protection."

A deep sense of peace flowed through Carl as he pushed the mattress over onto the floor and stood up, ready to face the day. Whether the war continued for a day, a year, or a hundred years was immaterial. What mattered, really mattered, was that he was where God wanted him to be. After all, that was the most important thing.

NOTE FROM THE EDITOR: Thousands of Rwandans perished during ethnic purges of 1994. Carl Wilkens left Rwanda when killing subsided and returned to the United States with his family. ADRA provided health care, clothing, and food to the refugees who flooded the border with Zaire. ADRA's activities have resumed in Rwanda, where its warehouse had been looted and destroyed. The rebuilding of destroyed homes and the feeding, health care, and relocating thousands of refugees continued for several months. Carl Wilkens plans to return to work in Rwanda.

17

A Warm Heart

Valentina leaned back, sighing. The enormous pillows fluffed up behind her made the old, hand-carved bed seem even more massive. The bed, which had belonged to Valentina's great-great-grandmother, was the only thing of monetary value left in the house. She was half afraid that it, too, would have to be sold, if indeed there was anyone left in Russia who had money with which to buy it. The rumbling stomachs of her son, daughter-in-law, and their tiny baby, Ivan, were much more important than any amount of sentiment.

She let her old eyes wander around the moonlit room, envisioning the beautiful furniture that used to occupy the now-bare spaces. An old crate in the corner held what remained of her wardrobe. An upside-down basket took the place of the ornate night stand her late husband had given her on a long-forgotten anniversary. Sometimes she was glad Petrov was not there to see what had happened to Russia.

After the collapse of the old system, prices had risen rapidly, industry and factories had closed, energy production took a nosedive, and mass unemployment and transportation equipment failures swept through the newly liberated Russia. Because the arts were still supported by the government, it was cheaper for a Russian citizen to go to the ballet (which cost about three cents in U.S. dollars) than it was to buy a loaf of bread (fifteen cents, or a liter of cooking oil, which fetched the exorbitant price of $2.00.

Valentina sighed. No, Petrov would have sulked in depression at the economic conditions under which the Russian people were struggling. How could it be worse? Her own intelligent son, Andrej, could not even find a job that lasted longer than a day or two at the most to support his wife and baby.

After the fall of the nearly seventy-five-year Communist regime, the Russian people had been left with a bitter legacy of chaos. It was hard to remember seeing the people smiling with joy at their freedom. Now these same people were locked in a struggle for life. Although Valentina had heard the reasons over and over again, she didn't completely understand them. Maybe Petrov, had he been alive, would have been able to explain it to her. According to Andrej, a breakdown in the internal distribution system, paired with hyperinflation and unemployment, had made food supplies uncertain. The average Russian citizen was faced with reduced buying power in an economy of rapidly inflating prices for all goods and services.

Their only income was her monthly pension, which was

the equivalent of U.S. $4.50; the infrequent jobs Andrej was able to secure; and, of course, the sale of the furniture at rock-bottom prices. They had managed to survive, although each day was a struggle.

Valentina knew that it was not only her family who suffered. Those hardest hit were many of their friends— single parents, pensioners, large families, and children. Why, just the other day, while waiting in a long line to buy bread, she heard that 90 percent of Russian children had vitamin deficiencies, and they were not getting vaccinated for diseases such as polio, diphtheria, and whooping cough.

A terrible state! Her thoughts flew to little Ivan. It was not yet time for vaccinations. But when it was, what then? There was barely enough money for food. Where would they ever find money for vaccinations?

Even though it was still dark outside, Valentina knew that they should be getting ready if they expected to be near the head of the crowd receiving rations today— unless, of course, the rumor was not true. Valentina shivered, but not from the cold.

Her good friend, Galina, had told her yesterday that a group called ADRA would be passing out free food rations to those who qualified. Galina herself had seen this food. In fact, she had worked for days in a great warehouse, repackaging the food into smaller portions.

"Russian soldiers transported the powdered milk to a warehouse near the city, where we repackaged it into smaller units for distribution. It arrived in huge fifty-kilogram sacks," Galina had said, her arms opening wide to indicate the size of the sacks. "And the vegetable oil came in twenty-liter metal containers."

"Powdered milk, you say?" Valentina had asked, her eyebrows arching in surprise. She had not seen powdered milk in—how long had it been? Surely, this was some fantastic dream of Galina's, and not the truth!

"But it *is* true," Galina had insisted, seeing the skepticism on the old woman's face. She had held up her hands. "With these very hands I helped to package the food into three-kilogram polyethylene bags. There were oh, so many I could not even count them. But," she had lowered her voice to a confidential whisper, "I heard there is enough to feed twenty-one thousand people."

"And they will be giving this away for free? This ADRA?" Valentina had chided with a disbelieving smile. "Why would they do this?"

"They want to help us!" Even now, Valentina could remember the fire in Galina's eyes. "You do not have to believe me, but tomorrow there will be free food, whether or not you are there to receive it!"

Valentina swung her legs over the side of the bed, cringing when her feet brushed the icy wooden floor. Perhaps this was a fool's errand, but she could not afford to ignore the possibility of free food. According to Galina, the elderly, families with many children, orphans, and single mothers were eligible first for the powdered milk, and then later for food.

She shuddered into her worn old robe and padded across the floor and out to the kitchen area, where Andrej and Ella slept on a mattress on the floor beside the now-cold stove. Valentina smiled at the sight of Baby Ivan snuggled between them, almost buried in the covers. Andrej had been certain that one of them would roll over on the child and suffocate him. It hadn't taken Ivan long to establish himself as the boss of the family bed, though, wailing loudly when either mother or father infringed on his sleeping space. Valentina had assured them this would be the warmest sleeping arrangement possible.

She shook Ella's shoulder. The moonlight shining through the window and falling on the young woman's long golden hair made it appear like silk. Ella opened her eyes sleepily. Valentina had heard Ivan crying once or twice in the night and knew that Ella had been up nursing him. There were dark circles under her eyes, and the shoulder Valentina shook felt bony beneath her grasp. She prayed that Galina was right and there would indeed be free food today.

"Come," she instructed. "We must be ready. The sun will be up soon, and we will probably have to wait a long time for the powdered milk, if the story is true."

Ella struggled into a sitting position. Baby Ivan rolled away from her and snuggled up to his father. Andrej moaned and muttered something in his sleep. Ella smiled. "He is dreaming of food."

"Isn't that what we all dream of?" Valentina asked. "Come, get up; maybe tonight it will not be a dream."

They bundled up as much as they could. Valentina waited impatiently as Ivan woke up at the last instant and had to be nursed again before they could leave. Ella wanted to bring him, but Andrej volunteered to stay home and watch him instead.

"Go, it is too cold out there for such a small one," he insisted. "We will play here today and wait for you to come home. Keep warm."

He kissed his wife and then Valentina's wrinkled cheek before they left. Sunshine streamed over Ekaterinburg, the capital of the Ural Mountain region. It glistened off the deep snow, sending thousands of diamonds glittering over the landscape. Galina, along with many other people, was already waiting at the distribution center when Valentina and Ella arrived.

"I am here only to see this marvel," Galina insisted. "I'm not eligible for the food, but I wanted to see the people's faces when it was passed out."

While they waited and a line began to form, Galina entertained them by telling all she knew about the relief operation that ADRA had coordinated.

"When ADRA learned that the American government was going to be involved in the relief effort to help us," she said, "they joined with the American Department of Agriculture to start a food-aid program here in the Ural Mountain region because this area has a severe food shortage. Together, ADRA and the Department of Agriculture brought forty-seven thousand pounds of powdered milk here by plane. After the milk, we will get vegetable oil, lentils, rice, wheat, and more powdered milk."

Ella's eyes lighted up. "Lentils," she sighed. "I have not had lentils in such a long time."

Finally, the distribution center opened, and volunteers began to pass out rations of powdered milk. As the line snaked forward, Valentina was impressed that the people maintained control, not pushing or shoving, just patiently moving forward. Steadily, they gained ground until finally it was their turn in line. A smiling worker handed one bag of powdered milk to Valentina and one to Ella.

As Valentina finally held the milk in her hands, tears crept down her wrinkled cheeks. It was true. It was really true! Here was the proof. She turned to Galina as she stepped out of line, Ella at her elbow.

"Thank you, dear friend, for telling me about this," she said. "To think, after all these years, to receive powdered milk again!"

Galina choked back her own tears. "I am so happy to have been a part of this," she replied, her eyes glistening as she smiled. "But it is ADRA you should thank. Now go home, and I will let you know when the rest of the food is to be distributed."

Valentina hugged Galina impulsively before taking Ella's hand as a safeguard against the slippery ice underfoot. The young woman's cheeks and the tip of her nose were fiery red.

"Hurry," Valentina urged her. "We must get you home to warm you before the fire."

Ella laughed, the first laugh Valentina had heard since they had moved in with her months before. "Oh, Mother Vetrova. I do not need heat to warm me today. ADRA has warmed my heart, and now I am warm all over!"

A Woman's Work

The young Bangladeshi woman timidly answered the knock on the door. A woman stood there with a friendly smile. Rohima bowed her head and stared apprehensively at the ground. What did this stranger want with her?

"Hello," the woman was saying. "My name is Nancy. I'm a women's development officer, and I work for ADRA. I'm taking a survey so that ADRA can help the women of the community. Would you be able to help me?"

Rohima glanced up for a moment, then nodded shyly. What could it hurt to answer a few questions?

Nancy asked questions about health, nutrition, and socioeconomic situations. Rohima answered as well as she could, feeling that her tongue was stuck to the roof of her mouth. She was sure her husband would disapprove of this stranger and all her questions.

But to her surprise, when she told him about the encounter, he did not seem to mind.

"What did she want?" he asked as he ate the rice she had prepared.

"She invited me to come into the community tomorrow for a meeting to learn about things that will help us live better," Rohima explained. "Of course, I will not go," she added hastily before he could say it for her.

"You may go," her husband said, after a moment's pause. "I see nothing wrong with learning about things that will help us live better."

Rohima glanced at him sideways, startled by his response until she noticed the faint smile on his lips. He was humoring her, indulging her curiosity by letting her see what the stranger had to offer.

The next day, Rohima found herself walking to the location the woman had told her about. She had thought seriously about not coming at all. What if she became interested in what was being taught, and then her husband forbade her to return? Maybe it was better not to learn anything at all.

She looked around skittishly. She wasn't sure what to expect—but it felt strange to be away from her home, where she spent all of her time. Even the smells from the market were strange because her husband did all the shopping.

Rohima learned so many things that day and on the following days that everything was buzzing excitedly around her head: how to wash her hands before cooking a meal, why they should drink clean water, the right foods to eat. She learned how to sign her name, how to read numbers, and even how to count money.

A Woman's Work

In the evenings, her husband questioned her on what she had learned. Rohima faithfully recounted every little detail, hoping that if he knew everything, then perhaps he would let her continue to go to the meetings. But he merely nodded and said nothing. He did not even complain on the nights she served healthful meals that she had learned how to prepare.

Some days Rohima and the other women who attended the classes played a game on a map of Bangladesh. During the game, the women answered questions about income generation. Rohima was amazed at how much she learned about her country.

After six months, the group had completed the training, and the women were eligible for their first small income-generation loan from ADRA. Gasps of excitement and pleasure rippled around the group. A sudden babble of voices broke out immediately.

"Ladies, please!" Nancy held up her hands to quiet the group. She smiled at them. "I'm sure you're all bursting with plans, and I'll let you discuss them in a minute. I only wanted to congratulate you. I'm so very proud of you all. The purpose of these loans is to help you increase your income. Eventually, you will be able to pay your loans back so that you will become independent of ADRA—just as a baby becomes independent of its parents. You're growing tremendously, ladies!"

That evening Rohima went home and thought carefully about what she could do with her loan. Some of the other women planned to buy chickens for eggs for personal use and for sale. Others were going to buy goats and cows for milk and to fatten for resale.

Rohima wasn't sure what she would do. Should she sell thatch? Grow cash crops? Deliver milk? Finally, she made up her mind. She would open a small produce stand where she would sell only the freshest fruits and vegetables, which she would grow on the public property beside the road.

When she told her husband of her plan, he agreed to it.

"I do not have a problem with what you would like to do," he told her. "Just be sure that your own household is taken care of also. It will be nice to have fresh fruits and vegetables to eat," he conceded.

And so the woman who had never even done her own marketing became a farmer. Rohima tended her little garden as tenderly as she would a child. The plants blossomed under her care, and soon her produce stand became known for its quality of produce.

One day, when she met with the group of women who had become like sisters to her, Rohima learned that one of the group members, a young Hindu mother, had died in childbirth. Her tiny baby, Litton, was left to die also.

Silence descended on the women after this solemn announcement. Then one woman looked up and spoke for all. "I vote that we use part of our group savings to purchase formula for Litton."

Heads bobbed all around the room, and murmurs of agreement rustled like leaves on a fall day. "But who is to take care of the baby?" a voice asked.

"I will," another responded. Rohima craned her neck to see who belonged to the voice. It was a Muslim woman. She should have been shocked. A Muslim woman take care of a Hindu baby? But among these woman who had proved that prejudice was no barrier to friendship, it did not seem strange at all. "I will take care of the baby."

"And we will help you," someone else added. "We will all take turns watching him so that you will not bear the burden alone."

Rohima could hardly wait for her turn to take care of

Litton. On the night assigned to her, she carried Litton home, hugging the little baby tightly to her. Suddenly, she realized there was something different. No longer was she frightened, as she had been in the past. Instead, she felt in herself a confidence she had never known before.

She had made new friends—Muslims, Hindus, and Christians, it made no difference. For the first time in her life, she knew what was best for her family and was able to provide it because of ADRA's help. She rubbed her palm on Litton's fuzzy head. He was being cared for because of ADRA.

She shuddered when she thought of what would have happened to him if it hadn't been for ADRA. Never would a Hindu baby be cared for by a Muslim woman. Never would a Muslim woman volunteer for the job.

"And I?" she whispered to Litton. "I would not have helped as I am doing now. I would have felt sad, yes, but I would not have helped."

She held the baby out so she could look into his big, dark eyes. "I am thankful for ADRA. Aren't you, Litton?"

The baby cooed and grinned, showing his gums. She inhaled deeply of his baby scent. "Because of ADRA, we have broken through many years of prejudice and barriers. And because of ADRA, you will live, little Litton. And when you grow up to be a man, I hope you will carry on the work of ADRA for your country."

Liquid Gold
to
Drink

Nwibe pulled himself out of the hole, inhaling deeply. Even the hot, dry air outside was a welcome relief compared to the unbearable heat and lack of oxygen inside the hole. He stepped aside to allow the next man to lower himself down into the narrow abyss.

Nwibe staggered over to where two other workers, who made up the team of four that ADRA had hired to dig the well, lay sprawled under a tree. He lowered himself with a groan, every muscle aching. He felt his body melt into the hot dirt beneath him.

The men rested, attempting to regain some of the energy that the heat sucked out of them each time they returned to the bottom of the well to continue digging.

Liquid Gold to Drink

Nwibe thought about the poor fellow down there right now. Even as he rested above ground, he could feel the oppressiveness of the hole, the way it blocked out the sun and made you feel like you were the only person in the whole, hot, dry world.

In the past three weeks, the men had become like cogs in a perpetually moving machine. Working in fifteen- to twenty-minute shifts, they had dug almost seventy-five meters deep. When they were finished, ADRA promised, there would be clean water, enough for the entire village.

"How far did you say?" Helmut, one of the ADRA workers from Germany, had asked when he came to view the hole.

"Seventy-five meters," repeated Nwibe.

"Why, that is equal to a building twenty-one stories high!" Helmut exclaimed, his eyes wandering high up in the air as if imagining the distance. He seemed very impressed.

"Have you thought about what this water will mean to our village?" Boube asked, bringing Nwibe's thoughts back to the present. Boube raised himself up on one elbow and squinted over Nwibe's prone body directly at the well, as if he could see it completed already.

Nwibe sat up with great effort. "Of course, I have thought about it, or I would not be crawling down into that hole day after day. I have thought of nothing else since we began."

And he hadn't. It truly seemed that every waking thought centered around that water. It would improve their whole way of life.

Still, it was hard to believe that soon, very soon, they would have clean drinking water. Clean drinking water that he wouldn't have to walk four hours to fetch and then walk four hours back home. Clean drinking water he wouldn't fight with camels and cattle for. Clean drinking water that would not make the children sicken and die. Clean drinking water that didn't taste like it had traveled through the entire country of Somalia before it reached his lips.

Nwibe brightened as Frank Brenda, the ADRA water project director, walked over to inspect their work. He began talking to one of the village elders of Mohamed Said.

"The men are doing a fantastic job," Nwibe heard Frank tell the elder. "The well will be finished very soon, and then there will be clean drinking water for the people of Mohamed Said."

The elder nodded sagely. "It is true. With the help of ADRA, we have accomplished something that I never expected to see in my lifetime. We are very grateful."

Nwibe gulped one last breath of clean air before lowering himself again into the hole. His fifteen-minute shift seemed to last forever. In the hole, time seemed to have no beginning and no end until he felt he could not last even one second longer. When he pulled himself out again, gasping, Frank Brenda and the elder were still talking. Nwibe dragged himself over to the only shade available. As he caught his breath, he listened to the conversation.

"We are so grateful for this well," the elder cackled happily. "We are so excited that we have decided to give you a wife when it is finished."

Frank held up his hands. "Thanks, but I already have a wife."

The elder cocked his head and studied Frank as if he had just noticed something unusual. "How many wives do you have?"

"Just the one," Frank replied.

The elder broke out in a big smile. "Oh, it's OK then. You can have up to four!"

Liquid Gold to Drink

Another ADRA staff member joined them and tried to convince the old man that Frank did not want another wife. They were ambling to another part of the village, still discussing it, when the digger had to return to the hole.

At last the day came when the well was deep enough. No longer must Nwibe look forward to endless days beneath the ground. Today was the day when he would witness the fruit of his labors. Today, they would draw up the first clean water ever seen in Mohamed Said.

It took two men to haul water up from the depths of the completed well. But ADRA workers told the villagers they would soon have a pump that would do the work for them. There would also be reservoirs to collect the water for storage. Villagers sang and danced all afternoon to celebrate the completion of the well.

"What are they singing?" asked Frank.

"Adam's song," replied the elder.

"Adam's song? What do you mean?"

The elder smiled and answered, "It's the song of the creation of Adam, the first man. God brought Adam to life. Now ADRA has brought our village to life. ADRA gave us new life. That's why we sing Adam's song."

Nwibe knew he would never forget the first sight of that beautiful water. The entire village waited with an expectant hush as the men groaned and heaved, drawing it from deep within the earth. A little water sloshed over the side before someone could steady the bucket, and a gasp shivered over the crowd. Not one drop should be wasted!

The water was treated like gold. Nwibe himself had a drink and thought it must taste like pure gold too. It was so sweet and clean. He had never before tasted anything like it.

Later, after all the villagers had returned to their homes or gone to ADRA's feeding program to get food, Nwibe sat

33

next to the well and let a feeling of satisfaction wash over him. It had been more than thirty years since there had been a well in Mohamed Said. ADRA had provided this well, and he had helped to dig it with his own two hands. It felt a little like having a big bank in town handing out money to whomever needed it.

The ADRA workers would be moving on now to put in wells in other villages. Soon liquid gold would be flowing in other places throughout the Adale region of Somalia. Nwibe stood slowly and began to make his way home. And in his hand he carried a container of gold. Liquid gold.

Banza's Incredible Journey

Banza Mukaley looked into the woman's tired face. She had been his next-door neighbor for thirteen years—his entire life. Right now, that didn't seem long enough. He wondered if there would have been a spark of compassion in her eyes if only he had known her longer. "I said, go to the market," she repeated slowly, carefully, as though she were afraid that he had misunderstood. "That's where you belong now."

"But— but—" Banza sputtered, drawing his thin body upright with indignation. "I don't *want* to become a thief!"

The old woman sighed, her thin shoulders heaving under her torn dress. "There is no help for it. After your mother died, your father was still here to provide for you.

Now that he is gone—well, I just cannot feed you any longer. Your appetite is so large that it seems you could eat everything in Zaire."

Banza knew that what the woman said was true, but his thoughts darted around desperately, seeking a solution. Maybe if he ate less, maybe then they could let him stay in the village. "Maybe some of the other neighbors—" Banza began hopefully.

"No!" The old woman's face suddenly became stern. "We have fed you long enough. You are not our responsibility any longer. Go to the market. You will be fine."

Banza watched the woman turn in dismissal. He stood there uncertainly. What should he do now? A sharp pain in his stomach reminded him that it had been a long time since his last meal, and it might be even longer until his next one.

He heaved a big sigh. The old woman's attitude was mirrored in each face he passed as he began to make his way out of the village. Clearly, they all felt the same way she did—he had become a burden.

Banza walked down the dirt road, feeling the dust squish between his toes. He did not want to go to the market. No one went to the market without becoming a thief. "And I don't want to be a thief," Banza said again. His mind whirled, searching for ideas of where he could get food.

"I know," he said suddenly to no one in particular. "I will go see the governor. Maybe he does not know about my father and mother and that I am all alone now. Maybe I can stay with the governor."

Banza tried to recall everything he knew about the governor. The only thing that stood out in his memory was that the governor lived in Lubumbashi. He twirled around a few times to get his sense of direction. He was going in the general direction of Lubumbashi already, he decided.

A farmer had passed him moments before on a cart that looked like it was held together with a little spit and a lot of hope, but even a bumpy ride would be better than walking. Banza ran to catch up. "Excuse me, but I need to get to Lubumbashi. May I have a ride?"

The farmer nodded curtly but didn't slow down. With a little running hop, Banza was able to make it onto the cart. He hugged his knees tightly, tugging his ragged old ski jacket down over them to cover up the holes in his shorts.

To Banza, it seemed as if the trip lasted forever. Finally, he dozed off. A lifetime later, he woke with a start. Something was different. It took a few moments to realize that the jostling of the cart had stopped. He looked around.

"Is this Lubumbashi?" he asked the farmer, who nodded again. The man cast him a quizzical look but still refrained from asking questions of his passenger.

"Where is the governor's house?" Banza's gaze followed the fellow's pointing finger; then he thanked the farmer and hopped off the cart.

Now that he was actually in Lubumbashi, Banza's sense of adventure was beginning to wear off a little, and he wondered about his boldness in approaching the governor in the first place. Well, maybe his idea was silly, and maybe the governor wouldn't help him. But one thing was for certain—the governor would never help if Banza didn't ask. So Banza screwed up his courage and went inside.

The woman sitting behind the desk at the governor's office reminded Banza of a little bird. She wore a bright yellow dress and smelled of flowers. Her hands fluttered around the desk, scattering papers, her tongue "cluck-clucking" as she listened to his story.

"You'll have to stay with the guards at the governor's palace until we find a place to send you," she told him when he was finished. But she smiled kindly at him.

Banza wondered if they really would find a place for him before he was old enough to *be* a guard himself. "I will try to get in touch with ADRA," the woman continued. "I think I may be able to place you at an ADRA orphanage at Bulaya as soon as it is opened. Would you like that?"

Banza nodded. That sounded fine. Following the woman's instructions, he made his way to the guardhouse at the governor's palace. Most of the people were kind to him but kept their distance. Banza wished he could talk to the nice woman again, but he didn't see her until she brought him a note and told him whom to deliver it to.

"It tells them to take you to Bulaya," the woman told him. "I hope you like it there."

"Will there be other kids like me?" Banza asked.

"Oh, my, yes," the woman exclaimed. "I'm sure you'll make lots of friends." She smiled cheerfully, but Banza noticed there were tears in her eyes. She gave him a quick hug before he set off to find the man who would take him to the orphanage.

When he arrived, Banza saw an old woman preparing a bundle of food. There was flour, oil, bananas, bread, and peanuts in it. Banza's eyes opened wide. What a feast!

"Madame," the old woman was asking a another woman, "could I have some salt too?"

"Grandma," Banza said, unable to stop himself, "you already have so much; you shouldn't ask for anything more."

The old woman burst out laughing. The man and woman helping her laughed too. Soon Banza was laughing with them. After the old woman left, Banza handed the note to the man.

He opened it and read, "The carrier of this note is the orphan of whose case you are aware. As agreed, we're sending him to you so you can forward him to Bulaya." The man paused and smiled at Banza. "So, you're the boy who is going to live on the farm?"

Banza nodded, wondering if that was good or not.

"You'll like it there," the man assured him.

Banza was so excited he could hardly sleep that night. What if no one liked him? What if there really wasn't enough food for the boy who could eat everything in Zaire? What if . . . What if . . .

Banza slept fitfully, but when he woke up to sunshine streaming into his room, all his doubts vanished with the night. This was the day he was going to the farm. He surprised his hosts with his bubbling enthusiasm and impatience.

But when they arrived at the farm and several people rushed out to meet him, Banza was overcome with shyness. He cuddled up to Bea, the wife of the nice man who brought him to Bulaya, and wished he could hide behind her. She gave him a reassuring hug. "You're going to like it here, Banza," she said soothingly.

He nodded and smiled, still clinging to her. Out of the corner of his eye, he could see some boys playing some kind of ballgame. Slowly, his grip on Bea got loosened until he was pulling away from her. That game looked like fun.

"We'll be back to check on you sometime, Banza," the man called after him.

Banza nodded, but his attention was now on the ballgame.

"Want to play?" one of the boys asked.

Banza nodded. He hardly noticed when the nice couple left, but that was OK. They had told him that they worked for ADRA, and ADRA ran this place. He would see them again soon. In the meantime, he planned to learn this game and eat food that he didn't have to steal. And maybe—maybe he'd learn something at school.

The Christmas Hugo Forgot

Doctor Hugo Sosa pushed open the big gate to the main ADRA clinic in Adale, Somalia, northeast of the capital city of Mogadishu. Bright sun reflecting off the ocean not a hundred yards in front of him forced him to squint. Closing his eyes a moment, he let the dry, hot air brush his face, smoothing the tired lines. For just that instant, it was easy to believe that he was alone, that this was any other beachfront in the world, and that Somalia was a peaceful place.

Hugo sighed and opened his eyes again. He didn't have to turn his head to see a burly "technician" standing just to the side and in back of him. The man was always present. Sometimes Hugo imagined he had always been there, like a third thumb or an extra leg. Something he eventually got used to and stopped noticing.

The "technicians" were necessary appendages in Somalia. The very word would have made him chuckle if the situation hadn't been so serious. It was really a polite way to say "bodyguard" or "armed guard." Depending on the situation, there were between four and ten technicians at the clinic at all times. It was a bonus that the technicians sometimes functioned as nurses and translators when it was necessary.

Since the beginning of Operation Restore Hope, ADRA had been assigned by the United Nations to work in the Adale area of Somalia. They had been working closely with a local nongovernmental organization called SAACID—a word that means "help" in Somali—because SAACID was familiar with the area and the people.

Hugo motioned to the technician that he was going to take a dip in the ocean. As he waded into the refreshing water, he let his mind play back over the events that had brought him to this place.

Born in Guatemala, Hugo had attended medical school in Montemorelos, Mexico. For a while, he worked in Brazil before becoming part of ADRA's medical team to Nicaragua after the collapse of the Sandinista regime. When the crisis in Somalia developed, ADRA asked him to head up a medical team there.

Arriving dusty and tired, having bounced around for what seemed like a lifetime in a jeep, Hugo began to attend to patients almost from the moment his feet hit the soil in front of the clinic. The twelve- to fourteen-hour days, six days a week, were exhausting.

The clinic was a renovated field hospital that had been looted and damaged after the government collapsed. ADRA had rebuilt it and added barracks to lodge the staff and to store supplies. Every day, the hospital saw between 150 and 200 patients, ranging from children with malnutrition to elderly people with tuberculosis.

Besides Hugo, there were some Americans, two volunteers, a nurse, and a few other staff members. Two Somali doctors and one nurse, who had been contracted through SAACID, also worked in the hospital. Together, they provided free consultations and medicines to the population of Adale and ten communities nearby.

Hugo remembered how hard he had worked with the village elders as he began to make weekly trips into the surrounding area to establish field clinics.

"I would like to make Adale the hub of ADRA's operations," he had told them, picturing clinics in the outlying communities that would benefit people who would otherwise have to travel for hours or days to receive medical treatment.

Now, ten rural clinics spread out around Adale like little satellites. True, most consisted only of a small room made with sticks, perhaps plastered with mud, with some sort of roof, along with a door and a sign to indicate it was a medical clinic. And inside there were a few rudimentary instruments and some basic medications. Each clinic was staffed full time by a person who had received medical training, and each was visited every other day by doctors from the hospital.

As Hugo emerged from the water and held his arms out to let the wind dry his body, he thought it ironic that getting adequate drinking water was a major problem despite being so close to a big body of water..

In one area, the people had to walk four hours to get water and then four hours more to get back home. Camels and cattle often competed with people at drinking sources, thus contaminating the water. This made supplying clean drinking water one of ADRA's top priorities for these villages.

At the hospital, the electricity was on for only a few hours every day, and that because they were fortunate enough to have a generator. All their water had to be carried from a water hole about five hundred yards from the clinic.

Hugo hummed a snatch of a hymn he was teaching the elders who came to the special meetings he held at the clinic on Saturday mornings. They were learning the songs in both English and Spanish, and, if Hugo did say so himself, they were learning very quickly. He smiled as he thought of the children who flocked to him. They, too, were learning the Christian songs. As far as he knew, his was the only Seventh-day Adventist church in Somalia.

In a small way, the laughing, smiling, happy children eased the ache in his heart when he thought of his wife and daughters, whom he was only able to speak with once a week on the ham radio. Trying to see them occasionally had proven quite a daunting task, one that he couldn't always accomplish.

The technician took his place by Hugo's side as he made his way up the beach. Hugo turned to take one last look at the ocean. As he did, he noticed for the first time lines of camels and big trucks patiently waiting for the cargo ships to unload wares to be brought into the interior. One of the ships anchored in the bay in Adale was a Greek ship.

"My friend," Hugo said, turning to the technician and smiling, "we are going to go buy some food."

Communication being another unreliable commodity, word relayed to Mogadishu that they were in need of food and medicines had somehow not gotten through, and now they had run out. Hugo saw the Greek ship as the perfect opportunity to remedy the situation. Possibly by this evening they would once again have medicines.

The compound in front of him reminded him of a hacienda. Surrounded by a tall brick fence lay the F-shaped building. The center courtyard was the main gathering area of the compound. The main headquarters contained a dorm for doctors and nurses and several other rooms. On one of the parallel wings were two examining rooms, a pharmacy, and a primitive lab. The other wing housed those patients who had to remain at the hospital.

Hugo gathered his things and made his way down to the bay, the technician following after him like a shadow. The afternoon was not cool, but a breeze blew off the ocean. A Greek sailor was just about to return to the ship, when Hugo caught his attention.

"Excuse me, but I am a doctor from the hospital." Hugo waved an arm in back of him, indicating the general direction of the clinic. "I'm afraid we've run out of food and medicine. Would you have any that we could purchase?"

"Allow me to ask my captain," the sailor replied courteously. He disappeared onto the deck and returned abruptly with a short, stocky, dark-complexioned man who glowered fiercely at them while the sailor rattled something in Greek, arms waving like the branches of a tree caught in a terrible thunderstorm. At the end of his lengthy recitation, the captain broke into a wide smile.

"Most certainly! You must take all the food you need for your hospital," he assured the relieved Hugo. "And I shall provide you with some vital medicines as well."

"Thank you so much," Hugo said. "Your kindness is appreciated."

The captain barked orders to a crew of sailors, who immediately sprang into action. As the sailors gathered the food and medicine, the captain leaned companionably over the rail of the ship. "It would please us very much if you would return this evening to celebrate Christmas with us," he told Hugo.

Hugo's relieved smile faltered for a moment as he suffered from a moment of confusion. Was it some Greek custom to celebrate Christmas so early? That must be it, he reasoned. He seemed to recall something of the sort. "Christmas, you say? What is the date?"

The Greek captain looked startled. "You mean you don't know? Why, it's December twenty-five, of course. We don't celebrate Christmas on the same day as you, but since we are the only Christians around, we'll celebrate Christmas again with you."

"I would be happy to celebrate Christmas with you," Hugo forced himself to say. The rest of what happened, whatever he might have said to the captain and crew, was lost to his memory. The next thing he knew, he was walking back to the clinic.

Hugo staggered to a sudden stop as waves of grief washed over him. How could he have forgotten Christmas? Tears filled his eyes as tender thoughts of his wife and daughters filled his mind—memories of Christmases past when they had been together, celebrating this precious day, the birth of the Saviour. The technician stood by, a silent witness.

Hugo had been so busy that he had not even realized he had missed Christmas. And yet, though he had missed the celebration of Christmas day, he was acting out in every deed the very spirit of Christmas. In the clinic, malnourished children received a second chance at life; mothers learned how to care for their infants; injuries and wounds were bound up. Over and over, health was restored, and life was renewed. Why, only that morning he had delivered a baby by Caesarean section.

He smiled at the thought of that baby. He was quite sure

that he could think of an excuse to hold it in his arms for a few minutes and reflect upon another Baby born years ago, One who brought the ultimate gift of healing to the world. Yes, there would be time for that and perhaps even a call to his wife and daughters before he returned to celebrate with the Greek captain and his sailors. How grateful he was for them—for their help and their fellowship. This was certainly turning out to be the most memorable Christmas he had ever forgotten.

Death
Stalks the
Streets

Hairon huddled against the pile of rubble at the far end of the cemetery. When something moved in the middle of the graveyard, his heart pounded with fear.

It was not ghosts Hairon was frightened of, but the death squads. Just the week before, they had caught some children who had taken refuge under a railroad bridge. Hairon had seen the children the next day, bound with ropes, tortured, then killed. The images refused to leave his mind.

While nighttime had never been exactly comforting (he usually went to bed with a grumbling stomach needling him with hunger pains), the terrible fear that now stalked him was new. If Hairon could have seen himself in a mirror, he would have been frightened by his own face.

His unruly, curly hair fell every which way, framing a face with eyes that were much too old for it. The dark circles under his eyes were mostly obscured by grime from the garbage dumps where he searched for food every day. Spindly arms and legs poked out of ragged clothes that had never seen a washing.

How long had it been since his parents had abandoned him? The days seemed to blur together into eternity. He couldn't remember the last time he had had an actual meal—not that there had been many at home. Comforts like that did not come easily where he used to live in the *favelas* (shantytowns) made of discarded wood and cardboard. Now he was discarded too.

Whatever had occupied the cemetery moments before moved on, and Hairon began to breathe normally again. His muscles relaxed as he drifted into a fitful sleep, disturbed by dreams of the death squad pursuing him.

When the sun finally rose over the city of Rio de Janeiro, Hairon pushed himself off the cold, hard ground. As he stood, dizziness washed over him, and for a few moments, he stood swaying. He was afraid that if he sank back onto the ground, he might never get up again. Gritting his teeth, Hairon forced his legs to begin moving. There would already be a crowd at the dump, taking all the best scraps from the day before.

He walked along, his hand clutching his stomach as the smells of food cooking in various restaurants mingled in the morning air. Hairon passed a young couple, almost falling into them as another dizzy spell hit him. His ears were ringing so loudly that he did not hear their question until they repeated it.

"The restaurant, do you know where it is?" the young man asked again.

"Yes," Hairon said, nodding. "Yes, I know where it is."

The man and his wife separated into four or five images as Hairon's vision blurred. He shook his head, trying to make the dancing images go away. When his vision cleared, the man and his wife were exchanging a look that Hairon couldn't identify. The woman smiled gently at him.

"My, but you look hungry. Would you like to join us?"

Would he like to join them? Would he ever! He nodded eagerly and led the way to the restaurant, his hunger spurring him on.

It felt like forever while they waited for the food. The young couple smiled at him, and Hairon smiled back. He hoped the smile looked friendly underneath all the grime. He worried that he should have washed up a little before coming with the people to this restaurant.

Suddenly, he became aware of the pointed stares of other patrons. Uncomfortably, he squirmed in his chair. He thought of leaving, but the hunger pains pinned him to the chair.

"Do you have family?" the man was asking him.

Hairon shook his head slowly. "I mean, yes, but not anymore," he replied.

"What do you mean, 'not anymore'?" the woman prodded gently.

"I don't know where they are," Hairon explained. "They told me that they couldn't take care of me anymore and that I was on my own. Then they left me and told me not to come back. I don't even know if they still live in the same place."

The woman looked as if she was going to cry.

Finally, the food arrived, and Hairon eagerly began eating. The nice couple didn't seem interested in the food after all and only picked at it while they talked. To Hairon, this seemed like very strange behavior indeed.

49

"Is it good?" the man asked, indicating the food.

Hairon tried to talk around a mouthful. "It's the best I ever ate," he replied sincerely. "The very best. Sometimes we get delicious scraps of food from the best restaurants when we pick through the garbage dump, even better than the food I had at home. But most of the best food is gone by the time I arrive. It takes so long to get there from where I stay."

"Then you have found a place to live?" the woman asked, brightening.

Hairon nodded and had another bite before answering. His stomach was feeling a little funny, but he couldn't force himself to slow down. It had been so long since he had a real meal in his stomach that he couldn't help himself.

"Oh yes. I have a fine place to stay. At the cemetery. There is a spot no one knows about, so I believe I am safe from the death squads. I have a bit of cardboard to lie on, so the ground does not seem so cold. And," he added excitedly, eager to share the news of his latest treasure, "I have my very own radio." He shrugged. "Of course, it does not work, but if I pretend hard enough, sometimes I think I can actually hear the music."

"The death squads?" the woman repeated, paling. Hairon wondered if she had even heard him talk about his radio. "What are death squads?"

Hairon shivered. "At night they are everywhere, looking for us," he explained. "Some people call them the Justice Committee, but to us they are death squads. You have to be careful where you hide. They go in alleys, abandoned buildings, empty garbage bins, under railroad bridges, everywhere."

"And when they find you?" the woman prompted.

Hairon swallowed hard, the images of the murdered children he had seen swimming before his eyes. "They torture you and kill you," he replied simply, unable to tell her what he had witnessed.

The woman's husband changed the topic of conversation, and Hairon forgot about the death squads and concentrated on eating. When he finished, there was a full, pleasant, somewhat rumbly feeling in his stomach. Warmth radiated all the way out to his fingertips.

"Hairon," the woman said when they left the restaurant, "how would you like to live in a home with other boys like yourself?"

Hairon thought of returning to the *favelas*, his first home. Then he thought of the cemetery, where he lived now, and the garbage dump, where he ate every day. *Home* did not have warm connotations for him, but at least in a home he would not have to worry about the death squads.

"I think I would like to live in a home," he told the woman. But the home they brought him to was no ordinary home. To Hairon, it seemed like a mansion; he had never been in such a wonderful place. The people, he decided, must be very rich. They ate breakfast, lunch, and dinner every single day!

"This place is called Xaxim Home," the woman explained to him. "ADRA supports it and takes care of the expenses so that street children like yourself can have a home and family. You will be able to go to school and learn a vocation. You will have brothers and a 'mom' and 'dad,' who will love you very much."

Hairon hugged the woman, tears in his eyes. "Thank you for bringing me to this place. Does ADRA live here also? I want to thank ADRA."

"You just did," she replied. "Now let's go meet your new family!"

The Farmer's Loan

The Thai farmer looked out over his rice paddy and heaved a sigh. Straggly plants stretched awkwardly heavenward. They were a weak shade of green, as if someone had painted them hurriedly in watercolor and left the painting to bleach in the sun.

Poor. That's what his crop was: poor. And that's what they were and probably always would be. His wife stood beside him, sweaty and tired, her shoulders stooped from working in the fields. They had done all they could to get a good crop, but the scanty yield only mocked their efforts.

"If only we had some fertilizer," the farmer said, pounding his fist into his palm. "If we had some good seed and some money to hire labor, we could get a much better crop from this land."

"I know," said his wife, bending with a groan to lift the smallest of their seven children. "But to buy fertilizer and seed and labor, you need money. And we have none."

"We could go to the money lender," the farmer suggested, knowing full well that they couldn't.

"And let him charge us more than 100 percent on what we borrow?" his wife asked incredulously. "How could we? What if something terrible happened and the crop failed or something happened to one of us and we couldn't work in the fields? We would lose our land."

"I know." The farmer sighed again. "Come, it's time to take care of the animals. There's no sense wishing for something that cannot be."

As he tended to the animals, he thought some more about the seven little mouths he was responsible for feeding and the depleted ground he had to wrest a living from. Already his poor wife was creating miracles out of the meager food supply they were able to purchase. How much longer could they go on? But she was right. They were barely making it now. If one crop failed—just one— they would be ruined. And who wanted to be in debt to a money lender if that happened? Things would be bad enough without that. If only there were some way to improve the land that didn't cost money. . . .

His thoughts were interrupted when a young man in a trishaw pedaled up to him, calling out a greeting. The man looked like a friend of his, but it couldn't be—his friend didn't own a trishaw.

"Hello!" the smiling man greeted the farmer. "Do you recognize me?"

The voice was the same. But the face was much happier than the last time they had met. "Yes, yes," the farmer said finally. "But how can it be? You were a hired worker. Now you have a trishaw? Do you work for someone else?"

"No," laughed the young man. "The trishaw is mine. I became a member of an ADRA project and borrowed some money from them. I used the money to open a small general store and bought this trishaw and took passengers. My income has increased from an average of two thousand to three thousand bahts a month."

"What project is this?" asked the farmer as ideas began to spin in his head. He could imagine his crop thriving, following the application of fertilizer. In his dream, his wife tended happily to the children as hired help worked side by side with him in the fields, sowing hearty seed and bringing in the abundant harvest.

"ADRA loans the money, but with the interest we pay—only 18 percent—and our savings, soon the village loan fund will be able to function without ADRA's help," he explained. "Then ADRA will be able to help someone else."

"Could I—" the farmer hesitated to ask. How could something so wonderful be true? Still, here sat his friend in a trishaw as proof. "Could I borrow some money? I would like to improve my fields."

"I'll tell you what," his friend replied. "Come and speak to the committee about it. Then maybe they will give you a loan when they see what you want to use it for."

The farmer was skeptical. True, his friend had received a loan, and look how well he was doing! But why would this group called ADRA loan money at only 18 percent when money lenders easily got more than 100 percent? There had to be a catch somewhere.

At the meeting, he met the committee composed of medical staff from the hospital, as well as elected group leaders from the village. The farmer looked with awe at the medical staff, for health professionals in Thailand are very much respected. He sat quietly until he was asked to speak.

"Tell us why you want to borrow money from the project," said one of the doctors.

The farmer swallowed nervously. "For my fields, sir. With good seed, fertilizer, and hired help, I could easily get a much better crop. The land has good potential, but my means are meager, and so my crop is very poor indeed."

"And so with the money you intend to improve your fields? How?" the doctor prompted.

"First, I will fertilize the land so that when I plant the seed, it will be properly nourished. Then I will buy the very best seed so that when it is sown, it will all grow. I wish, also, to hire some men to help me bring in the crops. With extra help, I could plant more and have a higher yield."

The farmer went on to explain a few more things he planned to do if given the opportunity. While he was talking, the doctor and other members of the committee watched him solemnly. He could read nothing in their faces.

"And how do you plan to repay the loan?" a committee member asked when the farmer had finished speaking.

The farmer wet his lips. It seemed as if he'd been talking for hours instead of just a few minutes. "With the increased yield, I will have enough money to pay my laborers, take care of the needs of my family, and also pay back the loan."

A long pause followed his words; then one of the committee members asked him to step outside while they discussed the issue and voted whether to approve his loan. The farmer stood outside, nervously twirling his hat. His family's future prosperity was being discussed in there.

Finally, just when he thought he could stand the suspense no longer, someone came to invite him back inside.

The farmer could hardly believe it when he was told that his loan was approved. Maybe now his family would have the things they needed. As he walked home, he felt as though he floated above the ground, so light was his heart.

Months later, as he and his wife brought in their abundant harvest, a yell caught his attention. The young man with the trishaw was at the edge of his fields.

"It goes well?" the young man called, as the farmer walked toward him.

"It goes very well, my friend," the farmer replied, looking with pride out over the beautiful fields. "We have a good yield from the harvest. We have plenty to sell so that we will have more cash. Now we will be able to take care of our family's needs. It will not be long before I am able to pay back the loan. I am so thankful that I did not have to go through a local money lender or middle man."

"It's all because of your hard work," the young man observed.

"No," the farmer corrected him. "It's all because of ADRA loaning us the money. I feel thankfulness in my heart for them each time I see my children eating well. And I thank you, too, for telling me about ADRA. Our family's economic situation is greatly improved because of all of you."

Miracle in Lipik

Smoke drifted in the open window of Marko Skorupan's house in Lipik, a village in Croatia. Marko, one of ADRA's drivers who delivered mail and packages from Croatia to besieged Sarajevo, leaned against the windowsill and looked out into the darkness. His body was tense, his stomach knotted. From time to time, shell bursts shattered the stillness of the night, sometimes followed by shouts or screams.

Marko sank onto the floor beneath the open window and clutched the curtain. What would become of his wife and children, now sleeping in their rooms down the hall? Was he right to have waited so long when others had already evacuated?

The work he had been doing was important, and Marko believed that God wanted him to stay and help. But what about now? Was it too late for him and his family?

"Lord," he prayed, "should I take my family from this place? Please, Lord, show me a sign. I want to do Your will."

The darkness wrapped around him like a warm blanket, and he slipped off to sleep. Suddenly, it seemed as if he were awake. In front of him, a ladder stretched upward. His eyes followed the ladder to where it pushed through an opening, from which daylight streamed, bathing him in a warm glow.

A man in brilliant white leaned down from the opening and reached his hands toward Marko. "Marko, leave Lipik immediately. Everyone else should evacuate too."

Marko woke up, a cold sweat pasting his shirt to his body. The full implication of the dream hit him: here was the very sign he had just prayed for. Quickly, he made his way to his bedroom, where his wife had been sleeping fitfully. Before he could awaken her, she sat up.

"What is it?" she whispered, wrapping her arms around her knees. She looked small and vulnerable in the moonlight, but Marko knew that inside she was strong and courageous.

"We have to go. I have had a sign."

She nodded matter-of-factly, as if this were an everyday occurrence. "I'll get the children ready," she said as the phone rang.

"Go," Marko told her. "I will answer it."

It was a church elder, Marko's friend. "We must leave." His friend's voice sounded panicky. "I have had a sign. A man leaned down from the top of a ladder and told me to leave Lipik immediately."

"I have had the same sign," Marko said, his friend's

words filling him with a humble gratitude that God would speak to them in this way. "We will come too."

Marko looked into the sleepy, frightened eyes of his children as they huddled around his wife. He knelt beside them, cupping their faces in his hands.

"Do not be frightened," he told them. "God has called us to come out of Lipik the same way He called the Hebrews to come out of Egypt. Now, I will be Moses, and you will be the Hebrew children."

"But, Daddy," said the youngest, "who will be Pharaoh?"

Marko pointed toward the open window as another shell exploded. "The shelling and shooting will be Pharaoh chasing us," he said. "Now we must hurry. There are others waiting for us."

They all held hands as they bowed their heads. Marko's voice quavered with emotion as he began to pray. "Dear Lord, thank You for this sign You have given us. We place our lives in Your hands. Please protect us beneath Your mighty wings. Send angels to lead us safely from this place. We ask in Your name. Amen."

A round of quiet "amens" followed his prayer. The family held to each other as they turned their backs on their life in Lipik, leaving all their belongings behind. As they left the house, a shell fell nearby, lighting the area around them as if it were day. Marko flinched. That had been close.

Marko's friend met them outside the house. "Quickly, quickly," the man was saying. "We must leave now. I have two cars we can use."

"And we will take mine also," Marko added. "Will we be able to accommodate everyone?"

"What does it matter?" the man asked frantically, waving his arms like a police officer directing traffic. "We will stack people in like cordwood, if necessary. Let's just get in and go."

The group crammed themselves inside the three cars. Marko sat for an instant with his hand on the key. Around him, the fear was almost palpable. Would they ever see Lipik again? Would they make it safely from this place? Marko took a deep breath and murmured a quick prayer for strength.

He turned the key, and the engine roared to life. Marko was driving the first car, leading the way out of Lipik. They hadn't gone far when the soldiers began to shell the little caravan. The deafening noise reminded Marko of a terrible thunderstorm. Knuckles white, Marko drove as fast as he dared over the craters and potholes. The steering wheel jerked in Marko's hands like a thing alive, challenging him to maintain control of the automobile.

At last, the shelling faded behind them. Believing that they were a safe distance from danger, Marko pulled his car over to the side of the road. On trembling legs, he got out of the car with the other men to inspect the cars for damage.

"Do you find anything?" Marko asked, running his hands over the metal. "Certainly there must be some damage."

"No, nothing," came the astonished reply. "Not even a scratch."

"God has protected us," said Marko's wife, laying a hand on his arm. "Let's thank Him."

The entire group sank to their knees beside the road. "Thank You, Lord, for protecting us," Marko prayed out loud. "Thank You for giving us the sign to leave Lipik and for sending Your angels to watch over us and keep us safe through the shelling. Be with us as we continue our trip."

As they stood up, Marko's youngest child pointed behind them toward Lipik, where a building had caught on fire. Red flames reached into the night sky. "Look, Daddy, it's like the Red Sea."

Marko smiled and lifted the child into his arms. He pointed to the road ahead. "And there is Canaan," he said. "Shall we go?"

The child nodded. "It won't take us forty years to get there, will it?"

Marko and the others laughed, easing the tension. "No. But you will probably be asleep by the time we arrive."

Marko stood beside the car for a few moments after everyone else had climbed back in. He inhaled deeply of the cool night air and looked once more toward Lipik. Maybe someday they would come back. Someday when there was peace. Right now, he was just thankful they had gotten out safely.

"Thank You, Lord," he breathed again before folding himself into the driver's seat and continuing on to safety.

Opportunity of a Lifetime

Meg, a volunteer ADRA nurse from Florida Hospital in Orlando, stepped outside the hospital tent, nicknamed M.A.S.H. after the TV show, and marveled at the instant drop in temperature. During the day, it reached over 100 degrees in the tent. The air outside under the scorching sun was a tepid 80 degrees by comparison. It was hard to believe that this same spot would plunge to near freezing that night. In her own tent were two sleeping bags, one stuffed inside the other, that she managed to worm herself into at night to keep warm. She chuckled to think that she had to come all the way to Turkey to find out what a wiener felt like.

Meg stretched and let her eyes wander over the landscape. Jagged, snow-capped peaks ringed the camp like a giant necklace of broken teeth. From where she stood, she could see some tents pitched just yards from the snow line. The sky was a bowl of blue so bright that it emphasized every scar in the ragged peaks.

To Meg it seemed a forbidding place for these Kurdish people to have flocked to. She wondered at the depth of the fear that sent them fleeing from their homes. According to the news reports she had heard, the Kurds revolted after Iraq's defeat in the Persian Gulf War. When the rebellion failed, more than a million Kurds had fled to northern Iran and here to Turkey.

After she had arrived at the Turkish military base in the city of Batman, which was operating as home base for the volunteers and workers, she learned a little about the Kurdish people.

"They were a bit like Arabic bedouins, always moving around," Jimmy, a medic, told her. "Except that the leaders have higher standing. They used to be nomads, but since the governments introduced sedentary agriculture and forced them to move their goat herds inside the national boundaries, they've had to settle down."

To Meg, the Kurds resembled other southwest Asian populations, except for the occasional incidence of fair coloring demonstrated around the camp. According to Jimmy, most of the Kurds had lived in villages and were involved in the farming of crops such as barley, wheat, cotton, and fruit.

She was brought back to the present as a crowd of children pressed up against her, smiling. "Hello! How are you?" they squealed, showing her their treasures: empty water bottles and other trash they had collected from around the camp. One of the Americans gave them a cookie for every bag of trash they brought to him. At least it kept the place a little cleaner.

Meg chuckled and returned the hug of one little girl she'd become very fond of. "Hello, Lucy. How are you?"

"Lucy" giggled, showing a gap where her front teeth should have been. The Americans had been giving the children English names like Henry, Jack, and Mary. Likewise, Meg dubbed this little girl Lucy. Although *hello* and *Meg* were the only two English words the girl knew, the language barrier didn't seem to be a deterrent in their communication.

"I see you've been busy this morning, young lady," Meg teased, hefting the three bags Lucy was dragging along behind her. "You're going to get a lot of cookies for those. Don't eat them all at once!"

Before she would leave, Lucy patted Meg's hands and pointed to her long hair. Braiding Lucy's long, silken hair had become something of a daily ritual. Deftly, Meg swept Lucy's hair into a French braid and tied it with a piece of string. The little girl surveyed the results with pleasure, looking into a piece of broken mirror she'd found.

Satisfied, Lucy let the group of children pull her away as she waved vigorously and called, "Hello, Meg!" until she was lost in the crowd.

Meg smiled to herself. There were so many unexpected things in this camp. The most unexpected was this feeling of contentment that swelled inside her. She had expected to feel useful, yes. Maybe even a little benevolent. But she hadn't expected this feeling of humble gratitude. Thankfulness at being part of the solution wasn't a feeling she had anticipated. Not in a place like this, so full of surprises and contrast.

Another thing that struck her about the camp was how friendly everyone was. It impressed her that the refugees expressed gratitude and made her feel welcome at all times in spite of the temperature, the weather, and the circumstances. And what was most surprising was that they all seemed resigned to what was happening around them. Most of the refugees just took what came.

The men seemed happy just hanging around, receiving food from the various organizations, being taken care of, and letting the women do all the work. It struck her as odd that not only did most of the men look pretty well-dressed, but they all looked clean. She herself hadn't been able to take a shower in two days, since the last time she'd been to Batman.

The women wore concerned looks, but no one appeared desperate. The people standing in line to see the doctor were the ones who showed the most concern, but it looked to Meg that many of these people seemed ready to spend the rest of their lives in this camp or another one like it.

She wondered if the harsh climate had refined their characters, forcing them to expect everything in the extreme. In this camp, life was reduced to the necessities—food, clothing, shelter, medical attention. Living, while not easy, had been simplified.

Behind her, the murmur of voices in the M.A.S.H. tent crept back into her consciousness. Her break was almost over. Soon it would be time to go back inside and let someone else out for a breath of fresh air.

The tent was a source of never-ending activity. Presently, they were seeing between two hundred and three hundred people a day. The main problem was dehydration in both adults and children. Mothers had become so dehydrated they no longer had milk for their babies. Generally, IV's were given, but if a baby would suck, it was given a bottle of formula. There were other problems, of course: parasites, vomiting, diarrhea, and an occasional illness like tuberculosis.

One of the highlights of the relief operations was the water system, which was now complete and working. It provided 250,000 liters a day of clean drinking water. Meg had cringed as she watched women washing clothes and carrying drinking water from the same stream. No doubt, the practice had led to much more activity for the hospital.

"Ahhhh," a voice at her elbow gasped. Meg jumped, turning to face Donny, a nurse's aid who had been working with them. He squeezed his tall frame through an opening in the side of the tent and collapsed against a tent pole next to her. "It's like a microwave in there," he moaned, dabbing at his face, which was red and splotchy from the heat.

"Donny," Meg chided with a laugh, "did you escape?"

"No, the troops sent me for reinforcements," he said. "They're getting backed up in there, and they want to know if you plan to come back sometime this century."

"Very funny," Meg retorted. "I was going back in just as soon as my body temperature got back down to 98.6 as it should be."

Donny squinted. "Not a chance." He looked at Meg thoughtfully and was, for once, serious. "So, what do you think of all this?" He swept his arms out to indicate the camp at large. "If you had it to do over again, knowing what you know now, would you?"

Meg smiled. There wasn't a doubt in her mind. "Yes, I'd do it again. I would never want to miss this opportunity for anything in my life. This has given me a satisfaction like nothing I've done before. I'm helping people without expecting anything back, and this makes me feel like I've never felt before."

Donny clapped her on the back, sending her staggering forward a few paces. "Good girl. You passed. See, we were all saying you should quit your job, extend your stay, maybe a month or two?"

Meg laughed. "You goof! Don't you get it? It doesn't matter that I have to leave. Someone will always be here to take my place because that's how ADRA works. There are always people who care enough to help out, whether by monetary contribution or by volunteering."

Meg took Donny by the elbow and steered him toward the conventional entrance of the tent. "Now, come on. We've got work to do while we're here."

Please, Mister, Save My Baby!

The young mother sat on the street outside her shabby dwelling, a shack made with scraps of corrugated roofing. It wasn't much, but, at least, it was standing.

Her home sat in the heart of Seven Peanuts, Haiti's worst slum. She did not need to raise her head and look around to know that. One deep breath was enough: the air was fetid from animal waste, human excrement, rotting garbage, and unwashed bodies.

The tropical heat seemed to beat the air down, smothering life and anything that was beautiful. Waves of heat assaulted her as she slumped there on the ground. But she did not move. It was the coolest place she could find. She tried to tell herself that this was all a dream, a bad dream.

When she woke up, she wouldn't find herself here in this place. She would be in the country, where things grew and flourished, surrounded by life.

She reminded herself that it helped to find things to be thankful for. She was thankful that the shack had not been made from cardboard, as some of the others had. She was thankful for the jug of drinking water that was left for her child. She was not thankful that the child no longer had any will to drink.

She stared down at her precious little girl cradled in her arms. Tiny arms and legs stuck out like little twigs from a bloated stomach. Flies danced around the child's face, alighting to crawl around before buzzing to a different spot. Her beautiful curly black hair had taken on a reddish tint, and her skin stretched ashen and gray across her small frame.

The little girl no longer moved when the insects crept over her skin. Her mother was too numb with grief to brush them away. What did it matter? Her child would soon be dead. "Odez, Odez," the woman wept softly. "Please, wake up, baby. You're slipping away from me."

She thought dully of her husband. Would she be holding a dead child this evening when he returned home, exhausted from the day's work? She knew her husband's every spare thought would be about Odez.

"You must go," a voice was urging her. She looked up from her grief-stricken stupor to see her neighbor. "You must go to the ADRA clinic," the woman repeated, placing a firm hand beneath the young mother's elbow and tugging on her arm.

"How can I?" the young woman wailed. "I have no money. My husband brings home one dollar each evening after working many hours of hard labor. Even if I did not buy clean water and food, I could not possibly afford to pay the doctors."

"You must go," the woman insisted, her fingers refusing to loosen their grip. "Maybe they will take pity on you."

Maybe her neighbor was right. Maybe the doctors at the ADRA clinic *would* take pity on her. At least she must ask. She must try. For the sake of her child.

The young woman struggled to her feet, gripping her child tightly to her chest. A quick jab from the child growing inside her reminded her that there would soon be another mouth to feed. But first, she must save this one.

The walk to the clinic, though not far, seemed to take a lifetime as she watched her baby's arms and legs flop weakly to the rhythm of her walk. She entered the clinic and approached a man in a white coat. He looked up and smiled at her. Swiftly, she spoke what she had come to say before anyone could ask her to leave or throw her back out onto the streets. "Please, mister, save my baby!"

The man took the child from her arms as a smiling woman bustled over and guided her to a chair.

"Sit," the woman said gently. "You must be tired. Would you like a drink of water?"

The young woman accepted a cup of water gratefully as she watched the doctor examine her baby. He laid Odez gently on a table. The child hardly acknowledged him as he palpated her abdomen and checked her eyes and limbs. Finally, the doctor brought the child to her mother.

"She is dying of hunger," he said softly.

Tears filled the young woman's eyes. "Her name is Odez," she whispered softly.

"I will do everything I can to save Odez, but you must also do what you can to care for this child and the one you are carrying."

The doctor would help her! Then her flicker of hope was strangled by fear. "But, mister, I do not have any money to pay you."

The doctor's brown eyes were kind as he looked at her. "Don't you worry about that. You just take care of your little girl. I don't want any money. Now I'll show you what to do, and when your baby is well again, you must bring her back for vaccinations."

A puzzled frown creased the young woman's face. "What are those things you are talking about?" she asked hesitantly.

"Vaccinations?" the doctor repeated. "Vaccinations keep children from getting sick or becoming permanently disabled. We give an injection that helps a child's body fight the disease germs and builds up immunity. So if the child becomes exposed to the disease, she will be immune to it. You see? Once your baby is vaccinated, she will not catch diseases such as measles, whooping cough, and polio."

The young woman listened intently to the doctor. She did not completely understand all that he said, but instinctively she trusted him. He wanted what was best for her child.

The doctor smiled. "I know all of this must be very new to you, but you will learn in time. Here at the ADRA clinic we will teach you how to take care of your family and keep them in good health. There will be classes to teach you skills that will help you find a job that pays better wages also."

As she left the clinic that afternoon, the young mother felt as though she soared through the streets. Because of ADRA, her children were being given the chance to survive in a country where many children never reach the age of five. Her head buzzed with the information the doctor had taught her. She reviewed his instructions for her baby and wondered what she would learn on her next visit. She rubbed her palm absently on her protruding belly. With the training she received from ADRA, this new little baby would have the very best possible start in a hostile country.

After tending to the baby, she set about cooking the food the clinic had sent home with her. Thanks to ADRA, there would be supper tonight. Joy bubbled up inside her. She looked out onto the dirty street; there was nothing different in Seven Peanuts. No, the difference was inside her. Inside her, where there had been nothing but despair and hunger, there was now joy and hope that tomorrow could be different. And with ADRA's help, tomorrow *would* be different.

Safe
at
Last

Amaradas put his hands on the floor of the cell he shared with twenty-five other young men and gingerly pushed himself backward. Groaning, he quickly took the pressure off his throbbing thumbs.

Amaradas braved a peek at the others who shared the small, dank cell with him. The sight made his stomach turn. Without the care of a doctor— He was afraid to think farther than that. He glanced down at his own injuries. So far, there was no sign of gangrene in his thumbs, but here in this place, under these conditions, it was inevitable.

He turned his head slowly, as if he were seeing everything in slow motion. In the corner, a man moaned and rocked back and forth, clutching his knees to his chest, his face flushed, his eyes bright with fever. In his delirium, he muttered the same words over and over. The man had been put in the cell with them only that morning, left to die just as the others had been.

Amaradas suspected that the soldiers had beaten the man the same way he himself had been beaten. He closed his eyes and tried to block out the sounds of suffering, the cries of his country being torn apart.

Ever since the Tamil antigovernment guerrilla fighters (Tigers, they were called) and their followers had demanded a separate state, Sri Lanka had been marred by fighting. The government leaders were determined to keep Sri Lanka one country. As the Sri Lankan army tried to quell the resistance in various locations, they were met with land mines, booby traps, and ambushes set by the Tigers.

When new fighting broke out along the seacoast, soldiers retaliated by rounding up all the young men from Amaradas's town, saying they were suspected of being guerrillas. Amaradas didn't know what had happened to the other young men, but he had been put under the control of an especially harsh officer. The officer had Amaradas beaten, kicked, and hung by his thumbs before finally being thrown into this cell to die.

Instead of dying obligingly, Amaradas prayed many times every day. Now he again struggled to his knees, shifting from one to the other to ease the painful pressure on his bruised skin. Ignoring his throbbing muscles and lightheadedness, Amaradas concentrated, trying to focus his thoughts.

The new man ceased his rocking and watched with wide, watery eyes as Amaradas swayed back and forth, attempting to keep his balance.

"What are you doing?" he croaked.

"Praying," Amaradas replied, opening his eyes momentarily to regard the stranger. "I am praying. Would you like to join me?"

The man barked a laugh, his eyes wild and shining. "Me? Pray? To God? Never! But you go right ahead."

"Thank you," Amaradas said. He proceeded to pray out loud, hoping that his prayers would bring comfort to some of the other prisoners.

"Oh, Lord," he cried, "please do not forget me here. Please save me from this place. Spare my life, Lord, if it's Your will."

"You, there," a voice barked. "What are you doing?"

Amaradas looked up quickly. An officer was standing at the door, peering into the cell. It was not the same officer who usually guarded the cell. The new prisoner stiffened and looked away from Amaradas, leaving him feeling very alone. The other prisoners turned away from him as if they had no idea who he was. Should he answer? Maybe he would be beaten more if he did. *What should I do, Lord?* Amaradas prayed silently. A wave of peace and confidence flowed through him. "I am praying to my God that He will save my life!" Amaradas answered.

The officer shook his head. "You don't belong here," he muttered. "I'll try to arrange for your release."

In what seemed like a dream, Amaradas soon found himself on a bus bound for Colombo, the capital. He patted the seat beneath him to reassure himself that he was indeed on a bus and not hallucinating in his cell. Amaradas had almost forgotten what sunshine felt like and how cheerful it made everything appear. He squinted his eyes against the welcome glare. No more would he be forced to live under the ground like a mole. God had saved him and released him into the glorious light. Tears trickled down his cheeks, as much from his overflowing heart as from the brightness of the sunshine.

"Thank You, God," he cried, making all the other

passengers turn and stare, but Amaradas barely noticed them, he was so thankful for this gift. The gift of life.

When the bus jerked to a halt, Amaradas made his way off the bus and forced himself to walk to the ADRA office. Many times the ground seemed to rise up to meet him. Over and over again he stopped to steady himself on the side of a building or some other stationary object. By the time he arrived at the ADRA office, he was barely able to stand.

"I am safe at last," he whispered, after giving a brief account of his story.

"Yes," repeated an ADRA worker. "Safe at last. It is indeed a miracle that you are here."

After his wounds healed, Amaradas realized that he needed a way to take care of himself. He had left everything that he owned back in the village. Now he needed to start over.

"Why don't you apply to ADRA for an income-generation loan?" asked the ADRA worker. Prompted by Amaradas's puzzled look, he explained, "ADRA will loan you the money so that you can invest in a business to support yourself. With your earnings, you will be able to pay back the loan, as well as take care of your needs."

"Yes," said Amaradas, "if I had a loan, I could start a business to support myself. I could sell vegetables."

After his loan was approved, Amaradas opened and ran a vegetable sales business until he found a more permanent job. One day he stopped at the ADRA office to talk to the worker who had become his friend.

"How is your business?" the worker asked.

"Fine," replied Amaradas. "I am so thankful to God not only for saving my life, but for sending me to ADRA to start over again. I feel like a new man!"

Terror in the Night

The rumble filled her ears. Natalia could taste the fear in her mouth, bitter and metallic, as she bolted into a sitting position. The darkness was impenetrable, but the crashes and screams that filled the night drew a horrifying picture.

Earthquake.

Around her, the house bucked like a bronco trying to jar loose a cowboy. Dishes that had been handed down for generations crashed to the floor and shattered, even as her life was now shattering. But Natalia's thoughts were not on dishes.

Where was Mikhail? Mama? Papa? Uncle Viktor? Hearing moaning in the other room, she began to swing her legs out of the bed. She had to get out, outside where it was safer.

First, though, check on the others, she instructed herself. It amazed her that her mind was calm and ordered, nothing like the chaos surrounding her. She lined up her plans like a list of chores to be done. No hurry, as if life itself didn't depend upon instant action. *Then we'll get to a safe spot. Papa will know which is best.*

Before her feet reached the floor, a beam from the ceiling fell on her legs. Somehow, through the blinding pain, she managed to remain conscious for a few moments.

"Mama!" she shrieked. "Mama! Someone, help me!"

They will all leave without me, Natalia feared. The rushing in her ears began to sound like a thousand locomotives bearing down on her. She opened her mouth, but no sound came out.

Natalia woke screaming, her body drenched with sweat. Someone in another tent shouted at her to be quiet and go back to sleep. She shoved a fist in her mouth to block the sound and looked around wildly. To her amazement, she hadn't awakened any of the other girls sleeping in the tent with her. No doubt they were all trapped in their own personal nightmares.

She pulled the blanket up around her chin and shivered as a cold draft sneaked beneath the covers and brushed her sweat-soaked body. The icy cold wakened her to reality in seconds.

It was OK. She was safe. She reached beneath the blankets to see if it had been only a dream. But her searching fingers met her twisted legs—and the horrible reality returned. The most devastating earthquake in the history of Armenia, the papers had said.

Natalia knew about devastation. After the beam had fallen on her legs, she drifted in and out of consciousness, not knowing how long she lay there. At one time she had thought she heard voices, but they were far away, and it took too much effort to call out. With a sigh, she had fallen back into a state of semiconsciousness, where it seemed she had always lived.

Natalia shivered inside the winter coat given to her by ADRA, along with the blanket and the tent she now slept in. If it had not been for ADRA, she would never have received the medical attention she needed after the earthquake. Without the shelter, she could have frozen to death, as so many of the homeless had. Winter in Armenia is bitterly cold.

A tear trickled down her cheek as the fresh memories overwhelmed her again. She remembered being pulled out of the wreckage of her home. Through the pain that enveloped her like a cocoon, she heard herself ask about her parents, brother, and uncle.

All dead, she had been told.

All dead. She alone was left. Natalia lay back down and tried to sleep, but her mind played the events of the earthquake back to her many times before morning.

A faint smile touched her lips as she remembered her own special nurse, Julia. One of the ADRA workers, Julia, had taken a special interest in Natalia. In the first ugly days following the quake, it was Julia who had coaxed food past Natalia's lips and had listened patiently as Natalia had recounted stories of her precious family. The stories and memories were the only pictures she had of them. Everything in the house had been destroyed, along with their lives.

"Never forget," she heard Julia say again on the day they had parted. "You will always carry their special memories here." She laid a hand over Natalia's heart. "And one day very soon, you will see them again." Her eyes shone. "When Jesus comes again. Never forget."

Julia's words repeated themselves in her mind like a lullaby. "I'll see them again soon," Natalia whispered to herself. "When Jesus comes again." Just before dawn she managed to fall asleep, and when she awoke, the other girls were stirring.

Outside, in the tent village where they now lived, voices greeted each other and the new day. The tent flap opened as one of the girls came in, teeth chattering from the cold. Her cheeks were ruddy, and excitement twinkled in her eyes. "Guess what!" she demanded.

"Katrina," one of the girls exclaimed, "you have found pastry!"

"No," the girl laughed and brushed off the disappointed groans rippling around the tent. "Something better. Something for Natalia."

The girls turned to look at Natalia, whose face was turning red. Although they shared such close quarters, she had kept herself separate from them. She was different— at least in her own eyes.

"Something for me?" she asked shyly. "What?"

"Do you know ADRA, who gave us this tent and our blankets and food?" Katrina waited for Natalia and the other girls to nod before continuing. "I have just heard that ADRA is building a children's rehabilitation center in Yerevan. There they will treat children who were maimed or crippled by the earthquake."

Natalia heard herself gasp. "They will be able to fix my leg?" she asked incredulously. She had lost hope of having anything in her life return to normal. Slowly, over the days that followed the quake, as she learned to adjust, to get by, she had accepted that she would live the life of a cripple.

Tears, which came so easily lately, spilled down her cheeks, and she turned toward the wall of the tent to collect herself. This was more than she had ever expected.

To walk again, to run, to leap for joy. All things she had blocked out of her future.

Little crippled girls without family or money had no right to expect that anyone, out of the goodness of their heart, would swoop down and restore them to wholeness. She had been thankful enough for the care she had already received. This, the gift of healing, was beyond her wildest imaginings.

Slowly, she became aware of the other girls chatting excitedly, and it struck her for the first time that she hadn't been alone in her suffering and wouldn't be alone in her rejoicing. Many of these girls had friends, brothers, or sisters who would also benefit from the rehabilitation center.

ADRA was giving her a second chance at life. A life she could face on two feet. Thankfulness filled her heart. Someday, when this was all over, she planned to study medicine. Since the earthquake, she had seen a desperate need in her country. Who knew? Maybe one day she would work for ADRA.

The Lion
and
the Lamb

Ivan Rios hunched over the massive desk that all but filled his cramped little office. The acrid aroma of antiseptic drifted down the hall, permeating the office.

Ivan massaged his temples and tried to concentrate on the paperwork in front of him. The hospital administrative offices were empty, except for the janitor down the hall, cleaning. Every now and then, Ivan heard a thump as the man moved something. That thumping was getting on his nerves. He was just about to shut the office door when a sudden rat-a-tat-tatting erupted that could have been the janitor banging on the pipes or the popping of machine-gun fire echoing down the hall.

Ivan fought his rising panic as reality dissolved. No

longer was he in his hospital administrator's office but back in a heated battle against the Contras. Smoke obscured his vision and made him cough. All around him the screams of the dying punctuated the air against the deafening sounds of gunfire.

Ivan turned at the same instant a shell burst among his unit. Dazed, but uninjured, he struggled to his feet, calling the names of the men in his unit. Machine-gun fire answered him, kicking up a spray of dust inches from his leg.

No one else from his unit remained alive.

"Doctor Rios?" a voice was asking. A hesitant, throat-clearing cough followed.

Ivan raised his eyes, trying to focus. The sounds and sights of the battle receded as he unclenched his fists and rubbed his moist palms on his trousers. He could feel the jackhammering of his heart ease into a more normal pace. The janitor waited patiently while Ivan's mind raced desperately to orient itself.

"Uh, yes? Can I help you?" he stammered finally, avoiding the janitor's penetrating gaze.

"I was just thinking it was such a beautiful day today," the janitor offered.

Ivan struggled to remember what kind of day it had been. Hadn't it been raining constantly since last week? "You like the rain?" He couldn't think of anything else to ask and wished the man would go away.

The janitor laughed. "Oh yes, I suppose. But I wasn't speaking of the weather. I was referring to the precious babies born today at the hospital. Babies are miracles, don't you agree?"

Ivan shook his head as if trying to clear cobwebs. Babies? When was the last time he had even considered babies? When had he last considered life? It was death that haunted him every minute of every day since he left home at the age of fifteen to join the guerrillas in the Esteli region of Nicaragua, who were fighting against the dictator, Somoza.

"Yes, I would have to say that every one is a miracle," he conceded at length. "Life itself is a miracle."

"Doctor Rios?"

"Yes?" Ivan wished this man would cut out the confusing prattle, say whatever it was that he had come to say, and get back to work. "What is it?"

"I've noticed that you seem very concerned about something," the man said, pausing long enough to be sure that Ivan wasn't going to interrupt him. "I wanted to invite you— That is, I think you would very much enjoy the meetings that I attend on Saturdays. I think there you might find some of the answers you are looking for. I think you may find some peace."

Ivan stared at the janitor thoughtfully for a few moments, making the man fidget uncomfortably. It impressed him that this man, who saw him only infrequently, read him well enough to know that something was bothering him. It impressed but also concerned him. How many others knew? How many others in more powerful positions, more dangerous positions?

"Maybe next time," he barked gruffly, shuffling papers on his desk to indicate that the interview was over.

The janitor smiled. "Next time then," he agreed before leaving.

Ivan rose quickly and closed the door behind the janitor. Then he slumped back into his chair, his head cradled in his arms. All at once he was that same fifteen-year-old boy again, scared and excited at the same time. How far up the ladder of success he had climbed since those days, and yet, in many ways, he was still on the first rung.

He had thought he had reached the pinnacle of success way back in the flush of victory with the guerrillas. He had always wanted to be a doctor and thought he was dreaming when the new government rewarded him for fighting by sending him to medical school. Soon after that, the Contra war started, and the government demanded that he join the war effort as a political officer during the summer breaks.

In school he learned how to heal people, but during the summer he learned how to destroy them. It was a strange life, this mixture of healing and killing. He returned to Esteli as a political officer of the government. Although he participated in several battles, he was never wounded. He had begun to wonder if he *could* be wounded.

After medical school, he was sent as a doctor to the Hospital La Trinidad in Esteli. There, he was the hospital medical director, the administrator, and the political officer of the Sandinista Party's local chapter. He ran the hospital and the party and joined the army in frequent battles against the Contras.

Successful, to be sure. Respected, yes. But still there was this dichotomy in his life. Like oil and water, they remained separate and distinct entities. He was beginning to suspect that it was impossible to live with them both.

Ivan shook himself sternly; this was nonsense. Silly, childish thoughts brought on by the babblings of a janitor.

"I've been working too late and too long," he muttered to himself as he collected his things and made his way home through the darkened streets.

Two weeks later, he was packing up some paperwork to look over at home. When he looked up, the janitor stood in the doorway smiling.

"Good evening, Doctor Rios," he said pleasantly. "Beautiful day, wasn't it?"

"More babies?" Ivan muttered under his breath. "Was it? I hadn't noticed."

"I wanted to invite you again to the meeting tomorrow," the janitor began.

Ivan hurriedly gathered up the rest of his things and looked up at the janitor blocking the doorway. There was no polite way around the man. Ivan shifted from one foot to the other. "I was just leaving," he said impatiently.

"This will only take a minute," the janitor promised. "You see, tomorrow is Saturday. Won't you come? I think you'll find real peace."

"It sounds like a good idea," Ivan agreed, more to get rid of the man than because he actually thought it did. "I'll think about it. Where do you meet?"

The janitor smiled with pleasure. "We meet right here on the hospital grounds, in a small room in the back."

"Well, we'll see, we'll see," Ivan muttered. "Now if you'll excuse me." He indicated the stack of work in his arms. "I really need to be getting home."

He didn't intend to go to the meeting. At least, that's what he told himself. Still, Ivan found an excuse to return to his office the next day to retrieve some additional paperwork. Before he could really toy with the idea of checking out the meeting, he was drawn to it by the sound of happy voices singing.

Singing, of all things! There was such joy in the voices, like angels in the heavenly choir. As if things like Contras and wars and killing didn't even exist. His legs propelled him forward without his actually being conscious of it until he felt the metal of the door handle as he pulled it open.

Smiling faces turned to greet him, but the biggest smile belonged to the janitor. Ivan was guided to a seat near the front of the room, where he sat enthralled by the proceedings for the remainder of the service. Not since he had left home as a teenager had he seen and felt such a sense of fellowship and belonging.

As he returned to his house, Ivan realized with a sense of wonder that for the first time he had not suspected every bush and shadow of harboring a potential threat. In fact, he felt calm and peaceful inside. The discovery came as a shock.

Ivan flattered himself that his weekly presence at the meetings was a secret, until the Cuban doctors who worked with him called him in to congratulate him on his work one day.

"We are especially pleased with your political work," one simpered. "But we are also very concerned about the meetings you attend on Saturday with those religious people."

Ivan swallowed hard. So they had been watching him.

"It's too bad," another observed. "We had plans to send you to Havana to work on a residency. Of course, if we did that, you would have to promise to stop meeting with those people."

The Cubans didn't seem to expect an answer, just obedience. However, for the first time, Ivan ignored what they said. What was a promotion without peace? What was success without hope? He continued to meet with the janitor's group and felt happier each time he did.

The next time the Cubans spoke to him, they greeted him with open hostility.

"It's this simple," a big Cuban hissed. "We would very much like to take you to Russia to learn better medicine and the latest techniques, but you must stop meeting with those people on Saturdays! If you don't," the Cuban threatened, "if you don't, you will have to be transferred someplace else or be demoted."

So, the demotion came as no surprise. A new doctor,

assigned by the Cubans, moved into his cramped office, and Ivan moved into even smaller quarters. Ivan heard rumors that things with the new director weren't working out, but he was so busy preparing for his baptism into the Adventist church that he barely noticed them.

When the director was finally released, the Cubans gave Ivan his old job back as director of the hospital, but this time he had no political duties—he had been dropped from the party. Ivan moved back into his old office and continued to run the hospital until the collapse of the Sandinista government in 1990.

When the new government took over, they invited the Adventist church to run the hospital again the way it had been before the revolution. ADRA would have to be involved, since this region had suffered more than any other in the country. So Ivan once more found himself back in his old job, only this time he would be running a hospital and healing people. Only healing, not killing.

When Haroldo, the ADRA director from the international headquarters, visited the hospital to assess the situation, he stood aghast at what used to be the best hospital in Nicaragua. The hospital had been totally looted. There were no medicines, no beds, no equipment. The walls were cracked. The floor was broken. Tiles were missing. Not a single door or window was left.

Haroldo bent over and picked up one loose tile and replaced it. Then he stood slowly. It was going to be hard work, but they could do it. They could repair the hospital. ADRA would provide medicines, equipment, food, and personnel. And when it was all finished, Ivan would run a hospital to heal them all—former Sandinistas and former Contra patients alike. And they would share the same ward. In this hospital, the lion would indeed lie down with the lamb.

The Man Buys the Farm

Eleven-year-old Marie stood outside the ADRA school in the small village of Bulaya, Zaire, and watched the evening wind blow across the gardens. The plants waved gently as if saying Hello to her. She waved back as her teacher came to stand next to her and admire the gardens. Marie smiled as she watched the sun sink lazily into the embrace of the horizon.

"You look as if you're dreaming," her teacher teased.

"I am," Marie replied. "Sort of. I'm remembering how everything looked before ADRA came and helped us grow the gardens on the farm and build the orphanage and school."

The day everything changed stood out in her memory as

if it had been yesterday. It wasn't long after her family moved to Bulaya, and the feeling of newness hadn't yet worn off. At first, Marie had missed her friends in their old village of Kikwanda.

Things were good in Kikwanda. There had been a school and health center built by ADRA. Here, there was nothing, not even food growing. In Kikwanda, there would be plants growing in the gardens. ADRA had shown the people how to grow gardens, even in the dry season.

She looked across the village to the place where she'd been sitting that day. She remembered tossing a pebble a few feet away and watching the puff of dust being carried off by the wind. She had been so intent on being sad that at first she didn't notice the white man. When she saw him, she recognized him right away. This was the same man who had come to Kikwanda! He worked for ADRA and had helped to start the ADRA projects. He was asking one of the villagers where he could find Chief Bulaya. Marie scurried across the dirt yard to where he stood.

"I will bring you to Chief Bulaya," she said shyly. "Come, follow me."

The man wiped his forehead with a bright red cloth. Marie felt sorry for him; he seemed to mind the heat very much. "It's been terribly hot," she remarked, hoping to make him feel better.

The man laughed a hearty, deep laugh that made Marie feel like joining him. "Yes, yes, it has certainly been hot." He followed her in silence for a few moments before speaking again. "Tell me, young lady, haven't I seen you before somewhere?"

Marie smiled. He remembered! She stood up a little straighter. "Yes, as a matter of fact, you have. I used to live in Kikwanda."

"In Kikwanda!" the man exclaimed. "That explains it.

The Man Buys the Farm

So, tell me, what are you doing here?"

Marie tried not to let her disappointment at being in Bulaya show in her voice. "My family has moved here. I— I'm afraid I don't like it as well as Kikwanda. But I would like it very much," she rushed on, "if you would tell them about the wonderful things ADRA did for Kikwanda so that they can do them here. Then I would be very happy. Although," she added honestly, "I suppose I would still miss my friends.

"That is where my family lives," she said, pointing to show him. She hurried her footsteps, thinking that maybe she was taking too much of the man's time. After all, it was Chief Bulaya he wanted to talk to.

Chief Bulaya listened intently to the white man, who said his name was Date Vanderwerff. Date told the chief that ADRA was interested in buying an old, deserted farm. Marie could hardly contain her excitement. Why, this was the very thing she had hoped he would speak to Chief Bulaya about. She stole a look at the chief, but his face was impassive. When Date finished speaking, Chief Bulaya did not say anything except to tell him to come back the next day for an answer.

After the man had gone, Marie turned to the chief. He was a powerful man, and she was afraid to talk to him. But when she thought of the wonderful things ADRA had done in Kikwanda, she was able to find enough courage to speak to the chief.

"If that white man comes, this village will never be the same," Marie told the chief. "In Kikwanda, people eat three times a day!"

Marie knew that because of the difficult times in Zaire, only favored families ate more than once a day. Chief Bulaya knew it too. He studied her face until Marie thought he must know it by heart, but he did not look angry, so she told him about the gardens, the health center, and the school.

All evening she wondered what Chief Bulaya would tell the white man in the morning. The sun rode high in the sky by the time the white man returned to the village to speak to Chief Bulaya. The two men met in front of the chief's house and began talking.

Marie stared at them from across the expanse of dirt that separated her from where they stood speaking in low tones. If only she could hear their voices. She was filled with curiosity. She had to know what they were saying. Before she realized what she was doing, she found herself creeping closer to where the two men stood, straining to hear what they were saying.

Hope filled her as their words became clear. They were talking about what ADRA hoped to do with the farm!

"We would like to teach the entire community about agriculture. Growing crops during the dry season will increase their income and quality of life," the white man was saying. "We'd also like to build an orphanage and a school."

Marie's heart leapt. A school! She would be able to continue to learn how to read. She watched as Chief Bulaya took the white man's outstretched hand and shook it, smiling. ADRA was going to buy the farm!

That had been months ago. Today she could hardly recognize Bulaya as the same place it had been before ADRA came. No longer was everything brown and dry. The green of the garden was so startling in contrast to the landscape around it that people couldn't help but look at it and admire it. It was like a beautiful green jewel in the midst of Bulaya.

Because of that garden, Marie didn't go to bed at night with a rumbling stomach anymore. That alone was quite an accomplishment, she knew, but thanks to ADRA, she could also read! This month she had won a spelling contest and been awarded a beautiful Bible. It was her most prized possession. She was already half through reading the first book!

"God has been very good to us, Marie," her teacher said. "Very good, indeed."

Marie nodded and reached out to squeeze her teacher's hand before the woman turned and went back into the school. Marie gave the thriving garden a last loving look and listened for a moment to the laughter of the children as they played outside the orphanage. Then she made her way into the school to help her teacher clean up the classroom so it would be ready for the next day of learning.

She had to hurry, so she could go home and help her mother prepare supper. She smiled broadly. Thanks to ADRA, there was supper to prepare and homework to do.